Table of Contents

INTRODUCTION

So, you want to explore the world of hydroponics? The sheer number of options to choose from—not to mention setup costs—can overwhelm serious hobbyists and commercial growers alike. Don't despair, though: it's possible to build your own hydroponic system in under an hour. That's where the Kratky Method comes in. Most hydroponic methods require pumps to circulate nutrient solution.

Others require air pumps and air stones to bring enough oxygen to plant roots. Most installations also require plumbing, big tanks, and lots of electricity. Rather than going the standard route, e.g. DWC, NFT, Bato buckets, ZipGrow, Aquaponics, and, Aeroponics, there's an easier way. The Kratky method is a simplified way of growing plants hydroponically.

The process involves placing your plants in jars or containers with a nutrient dense solution of water without the use of water pumps and aeration. The plants are suspended above the water and are sealed off from open air to allow for root growth that reaches towards the water below. The Kratky Method was developed by University of Hawaii researcher Bernard Kratky as a self-contained system.

He and his colleagues experimented with cucumber plants grown in plastic trash bins in 2000 before moving on to lettuces in 2009. It's elegant in its simplicity. Plants in hydro need nutrient solution at their roots but they also need to breath. Most active systems supply that air with machines of one kind or another. In this method however the plants themselves provide their oxygen in a roundabout way.

Plants are placed in a sealed container of nutrient solution with their roots more or less dangling below. As the plant shoots up it uses the water in the reserve and gradually exposes the roots, allowing them a perfect balance of water and oxygen. By the time the reserve is dry it's ready for harvest. Homegrown lettuce in the dead of winter or the heat of late summer? It's possible with hydroponics.

And you don't need a fancy setup with electric pumps and a water circulation system. The Kratky method lets you do it with a grow light and an empty coffee bin. Read on to find out more!

THE ULTIMATE GUIDE ON KRATKY

HYDROPONICS

Growing your favorite plants, herbs, and flowers in hydroponic systems has many advantages, including indoor growing and exclusion of soil-bourne diseases. However, some systems might be a bit too complex for beginners and require a lot of your attention. Good news though, we might have a solution for you in the simplest form of hydroponics yet – Kratky hydroponics!

AThe Kratky method is easy to set up for your indoor garden, and the best thing is that it's a passive method. It doesn't require an air stone, any electric devices, or air pumps. So, if you would like to learn how the Kratky method works to have a high yield in an effortless way of gardening, stay tuned!

How Does Kratky Hydroponics Work?

Growing plants with the Kratky method is arguably the most straightforward way of hydroponic gardening, and it's also the easiest one to get a grasp of. One of its main advantages, when compared to recirculating hydroponic systems, is that you don't have to change the nutrient solution, or refill the tank. So, you'll be pre-calculating the needed water and nutrient solution for the entire growth cycle of the plant.

The beauty of this system is how the plants receive their needed share of oxygen and expand their roots. As plants are placed on top of the growth container in net pots, their roots start absorbing the nutrient solution in the reservoir below the lid. As the plants grow, their roots will start drinking up the nutrients and therefore lower the water level in the reservoir.

At this point, there will be a layer of air in the upper section of the reservoir and the roots will get enough aeration. It's the golden combination of hydroponics to create a pocket of moist air to oxygenate the roots, while still feeding them with the nutrient solution below. The Kratky hydroponic system takes care of everything for you, so with the addition of time, your plant will get everything it needs for steady growth.

Once the water level reduces and the air pocket is created, the plant's roots will extend downwards to reach the nutrients. So, it entices an extremely fast growth, especially with leafy greens. You can grow all sorts of plants with Kratky hydroponics – from leafy greens to herbs, mints, and veggies like tomatoes. You just need to adjust the system in terms of the reservoir size and amount of nutrient water needed for the growth cycle of different plants.

Setting up The Kratky Method Components

Before you start growing plants with the Kratky method, it's time for us to deal with building the system. Luckily, it's fairly easy to set up this form of a hydroponic system, so let's jump straight into the needed items:

- ✓ Nutrient reservoir
- ✓ Net pots
- ✓ Lid
- ✓ Nutrients
- ✓ Growing medium

With the Kratky hydroponic growing method, you won't need to bother using all the air pumps, tubing, timers, and similar equipment. So, let's get into how building the system works by starting with the most important aspect – the growth tank.

Getting The Reservoir Ready

The size of your reservoir is the most important thing since once you get all the nutrients and water in, there's no refilling the tank. So, make sure to consider the needs of specific types of plants and how much nutrient water they'll need to properly develop. For example, you can use a mason jar for something as small as herbs. However, chances are that you'll need a proper growth container for larger plants.

One option that I'd certainly recommend is getting a 5-gallon bucket from Home Depot. Now, once you've got the buckets, you'll also have to make a proper mix of hydroponic fertilizer depending on the plant type and place the seedling of your plant into a net pot with a growing medium.

Net Cups – Perfect For The Kratky Method

To make sure that your plant grows properly in this system, you'll have to get a net cup. As we said, you'll be placing the seedling in a net cup filled with a growing media to give it enough stability, and to allow the roots through to reach the nutrient water below.

Hydroponics Growing Lettuce, Basil And Cilantro

You can find net cups in your local gardening store or online and there are different sizes for different types of plants. You might want to gently pull the roots through the holes at the bottom of net cups, so they can expand downwards without being intertwined.

Why Is The Lid Important?

Logically, the lid serves to hold the plant's cup in place on top of the nutrient container. However, it also serves a different purpose in the Kratky method. It prevents the nutrient solution evaporation and creates a closed system. The usual lid type for the Kratky hydroponic system is just an ordinary plastic lid.

You can also use a styrofoam lid which creates good isolation so the air gap below it remains moist enough once the plant's roots start drinking up the water.

Water and Nutrients

The Kratky method works well with any sort of nutrient solution, and different NPK ratios and ingredients depend on the plants entirely. To set up the system, you'll need to put the effort into calculating the amount of water and nutrient solution that your plant needs. It's probably the trickiest thing about the Kratky method, and you should carefully calculate the water amount and nutrients as you won't be adding more throughout the process.

You must allow the lower section of the net pot to be completely under the water level. Because of this, you'll entice the seedling roots to grow, as the nutrients are transferred through the growing medium initially. The water level will decline over time as the nutrients are absorbed by the roots.

Best Growing Media To Use With the Kratky Method

Along with the diversity of hydroponic nutrients that go well with the Kratky method, you can also count on a wide array of growing mediums. One growing medium that's particularly convenient for Kratky hydroponics is coconut coir, as it's pH neutral and extremely stable to support the seedlings. You can also use Rockwool, clay pebbles, and perlite – the choice is completely up to you.

You should place the seedlings directly into net pots filled with a growing medium of your choice to make this hydroponic system sustainable for undeveloped plants. As the plants grow, you'll find the roots expanding deep towards the bottom of the tank. Even at this point, the growing mediums still serve a crucial role in the system as they hold the plant and the roots in place.

Best Plants To Grow With Kratky Hydroponics

The Kratky method is perfect if you want to grow plants indoors, but depending on the size of your system, you might be able to grow even larger plants with extremely high yields. After all, this method is even used in commercial growing, even though it's not as frequent in this agriculture sector as aquaponics and NFT hydroponics. So, if you want to know about the best fruiting plants and veggies to grow with the Kratky method, here's a list of a few of the best options:

- ✓ Spinach
- ✓ Kale
- ✓ Cherry tomatoes
- ✓ Lettuce
- ✓ Chives
- ✓ Sage
- ✓ Basil
- ✓ Collard greens

- ✓ Cucumbers
- ✓ Broccoli
- ✓ Spring onions

Now, you'll have to understand the nature of the Kratky method to get a bigger picture of what you can grow with it. Leafy greens and small veggies and herbs that don't require much water are perfect options. However, you might have a bit of an issue with cucumbers, onions, and root vegetables that need more water and more space for the roots to expand. However, if you buy a container that's large enough and pre-calculate the amount of water and nutrients needed, it's possible to grow larger tomatoes than just cherry species, along with cucumbers and even carrots!

Why Is It The Best Method For Home Growers?

The Kratky system is just pure joy for those who might be a bit lazy or just don't have enough time to constantly check on the system. Once you set it up, there are no additional worries that come along until the fruiting season.

Home Kratky Method Of Hydroponics

Growing basil, parsley, and watercress herbs in Kratky Hydroponic system. Even after the harvest, you can still use the same system for planting more veggies and herbs. Just remember to occasionally wipe the system clean and wash it after a few growing cycles.

Kratky Hydroponics Nutrients Guide: Salts, Liquids, and More

The Kratky method is a simple hydroponic system that requires no power, pumps, or moving parts. The most common Kratky setup utilizes a reservoir (5-gallon buckets, Mason jars, or other repurposed items) that holds a nutrient solution. The plant is suspended in a net cup above the solution. And that's it! While most of the components can be sourced from around your home or the local big-box store, proper Kratky hydroponics nutrients can be hard to find.

If you don't have a specialty hydroponic store in your area, you will have to make an online order—but with all of the available options, how do you know which ones will work? Luckily, plants are not too picky and will adapt to a wide variety of nutrient solutions. Let's take a look at the three most common options for Kratky hydroponics nutrients: liquid, dry, and compost tea.

Dry Nutrients

Dry nutrients (also referred to as soluble or salt nutrients) are the industry standard for hydroponic nutrient solutions. Most cultivators who grow regularly will tend to gravitate towards dry nutrients, as they are cheaper and lighter weight. Shipping costs are cheaper and storing the product is easier. The holy grail of Kratky hydroponics nutrients is the MasterBlend formula.

While much of the Kratky method is still evolving as people continue to experiment, one thing is for sure: you will experience quality results if you use the proper MasterBlend ratio. There may still be room for improvement, but it is an excellent standard of quality. While other dry nutrients are certainly available, MasterBlend has been tested extensively by YouTubers and do-it-yourselfers.

The most common MasterBlend ratio is as follows:

- ✓ 1 Gallon of Water
- ✓ 2g of MasterBlend 4-18-38
- ✓ 1g Magnesium Sulfate (Epsom Salt)
- ✓ 2g Calcium Nitrate (15.5-0-0)

The nutrients MUST be mixed in a specific order. First, dissolve the MasterBlend into the water. Then, add the magnesium sulfate. Finally, mix in the calcium nitrate. Be sure that each nutrient is fully dissolved before adding the next one. The recipe can be scaled up or down, depending on the size of your reservoir. When prepping multiple reservoirs, it is always advised to mix the solution in larger batches to promote consistency between your solutions.

Liquid Nutrients

Most hydroponic beginners gravitate towards liquid nutrients. They are simple and effective and require no mixing. However, convenience comes with a cost—liquid nutrients are the most expensive option on our list. To put it simply, liquid nutrients are just premixed versions of dry nutrients, so you are paying extra for someone else to do the mixing for you. To promote luscious leafy growth, start your plants with a liquid nutrient that is crafted for the 'vegetative' stage.

These usually have a relatively balanced NPK ratio (for example, FoxFarm's Grow Big® Liquid Plant Food has an NPK ratio of 6-4-4). Lettuce and other greens can be kept on this regimen from seed to harvest. For plants that put off fruit, you may want to switch to a nutrient solution that promote flower and fruit development (although this is not strictly necessary).

These solutions will have a higher level of phosphorus (for example, FoxFarm's Tiger Bloom® Liquid Plant Food has an NPK ratio of 2-8-4). The measurements and ratios will differ depending on the specific product you use, so follow the bottle's directions. If you choose to use liquid solutions for your Kratky hydroponics nutrients, check out these tried and true products (for the record, I do not earn a commission on these links—I am just recommending quality products that are popular in the industry):

- ✓ FoxFarm Liquid Trio Pack
- ✓ General Hydroponics FloraSeries
- ✓ Compost Tea

The Kratky method is the perfect off-grid growing solution, as no power or complicated equipment are needed. Many people who are interested in

Kratky hydroponics may have access to a free source of nutrients: compost! This method may take some experimentation, as you will never be able to measure the exact amount of nutrients in your compost tea—but who cares! The method is free and eco-friendly, so try out a few different ratios until you find the sweet spot.

Here is a simple recipe for compost tea:

✓ 2 Cups Finished Compost
✓ 5 Gallons of Non-Chlorinated Water

And that's it!

Allow the compost tea to sit for at least 24 hours. Strain the liquid and you will have yourself a potent nutrient solution. Additional additives can include molasses, kelp meal, or fish fertilizer.

7 Crucial Things to Know About the Kratky Method of Gardening

The Kratky method is a form of hydroponics that is adaptable for small home gardens or large-scale production. Here are a few things to know about this simple technique. Hydroponics offers some advantages for plants that grow well in water. It seems counterintuitive, but hydroponics actually uses less water than growing plants in soil. It's possible to grow more in less space, and because the gardener can control the nutrients, plants usually grow faster.

Kratky method hydroponics was developed by Bernard Kratky, a researcher at the University of Hawaii in the 1990s. The non-recirculating hydroponic Kratky method does not require pumps, electricity, or wicks. Instead, plants sit atop a "raft"—a netted pot containing a growing medium—that is fixed to the top of a small container or tank and filled with nutrient solution. As the plant grows, the nutrient solution level decreases to allow for air space.

1. The Kratky method is a form of passive hydroponics.

Considered a passive method because it doesn't require pumps to circulate water and nutrients, Kratky hydroponics relies on a stagnant hydroponic solution and air space. Air stones and wicks are unnecessary. There's no need to change out the water, nor is there a concern about rejuvenating oxygen for the plants. As the plant grows, the water level drops, creating air space for the roots.

When the plant is ready for harvest, the nutrient-filled water is nearly used up. It does not need replenishing; gardeners calculate the amount of solution needed by the plants and fill the tank only once. After the plant is harvested, the gardener can refill the tank and place new transplants on top of the tank to start another crop. After three to five growing cycles, the tank should be cleaned.

2. Kratky hydroponics requires five basic supplies.

The DIY Kratky method is inexpensive and requires only the following supplies to get started:

- ✓ Container. Depending on the size of the plant, you can start with something as small as a mason jar. Many gardeners opt for something larger, such as a 5-gallon bucket. Large-scale production might require a tank.
- ✓ Lid. The lid is very important in preventing evaporation of the nutrient solution and in supporting the plant above the water. Plastic or Styrofoam are suitable materials.
- ✓ Net pots. The webbed, plastic hydroponic growing container with holes in the bottom allows the nutrients to reach the roots and the solution to drain. These are essential to successfully growing plants hydroponically.
- ✓ Growing medium. The plants will need a pH-neutral growing medium, such as

coconut fiber (a sustainable, organic, biodegradable medium made from shredding the inner pith of coconut husks), rockwool (or stonewool, which is a porous material made of spun basalt rock fibers), lightweight expanded clay aggregate (or clay pebbles, which are round pieces of heat-expanded clay), or perlite (a lightweight volcanic rock).

✓ Hydroponic fertilizer. Kratky method fertilizer is a mixture of Masterblend fertilizer, calcium nitrate, and magnesium sulfate in a 4-18-38 ratio. The amount must be carefully calculated to suit the size of the container and/or level of water.

3. You must calculate the amount of water and nutrients for the plant's entire growth cycle at the beginning.

As opposed to the procedure used in recirculating hydroponic systems, the Kratky method does not require additional supplementation of water and nutrients during the growing period. Instead, the grower fills the container with enough water and nutrients to last the plant's lifespan. At initial setup, the bottom one-third of the net pot should be covered in water and Kratky hydroponics nutrients to keep the growing medium wet.

The plant will take up the water as it grows, but as the water level declines, the plant's roots will grow, continuing to reach the nutrient solution. You must carefully calculate the amount of water and nutrients to account for the size of the container for effective growth.

4. An opaque reservoir container is best.

Opaque containers prevent sunlight from reaching a plant's roots. The importance of this for hydroponic growing is to inhibit harmful algae and bacteria growth. Algae robs the water of nutrients and oxygen. If the plant fails to take up these vital substances due to algae growth, the plant will eventually die. It's possible to use a 2-liter soda bottle, milk jug, or even a mason jar like the one shown below (available at Etsy) for the Kratky method.

However, if the container is clear, wrap it with opaque tape or paper to block sunlight.

5. Grow different types of plant in separate containers.

Because different plants have varying growth rates and nutritional demands, it's best to grow a mono crop in each container. Grown together, deep-rooted vigorous growers like bok choy will starve out tender leaf lettuce because lettuce doesn't grow as quickly and will eventually lose out. The lettuce must compete with the bok choy for nutrient water as the reservoir level declines, and the rapidly growing bok choy soaks up water faster than the lettuce does.

It may be possible to grow similar plants together if the plants have similar requirements. But if the lid supporting the net pots is slightly crooked, one plant could have more access to the nutrient water than the other, potentially outcompeting it.

6. Leafy greens and herbs grow well with Kratky method hydroponics.

Although some houseplants grow well hydroponically, the plants most commonly—and successfully—grown with the Kratky method are leafy greens and herbs. This method is not generally suitable for flowering or fruiting plants, which require additional nutrients to produce fruit. Leaf crops are best for this hydroponic growing method; most leafy greens and herbs are small and fast-growing plants.

For example, lettuce is one of the easiest plants to grow with Kratky hydroponics, thanks to its fast growth rate and high yield. Spinach and celery also grow quickly and do well in Kratky hydroponic setups. Basil and oregano are some of the easier herbs to grow hydroponically.

7. Large, thirsty plants like tomatoes and root vegetables like potatoes are not well suited for the Kratky method.

Not all plants are ideally suited to be grown using the Kratky method. Flowering and fruiting plants typically need additional nutrients for production, and some plants are especially "thirsty." To help determine if a plant is suitable for hydroponic growth, you can use an app to learn about plant care.

Tomatoes, for instance, are very thirsty plants; they need energy to produce those juicy fruits. Tomatoes also require a large container for their roots, and the container would likely require regular refilling, due in part to the extended time it takes to get to harvest. In addition, the pH must hit a very specific range, as must the water temperature.

Tomatoes also require a tremendous amount of light. Root crops such as carrots, turnips, potatoes, and beets grow below the soil (in this case, water) line and don't do well in Kratky hydroponic systems. Potatoes are susceptible to root rot. Carrots cannot grow successfully in net cups because the cups will restrict their growth. However, if you want access to fresh leafy greens and herbs, the Kratky method is an easy solution.

Frequently Asked Questions (FAQ)

What can you grow with the Kratky method?

With the Kratky method, you can grow various kinds of smaller plants that don't require much space for root spreading and water. So, some of the best options include leafy greens, cherry tomatoes, and herbs.

How often do you change the water in the Kratky method?

One of the best things about the Kratky method of hydroponics is that you don't have to change the water during the growing cycle. Gardeners should pre-calculate the amount of water and nutrients needed, and the water level should be nearly dried out as the growing cycle reaches its end.

What do you need for Kratky hydroponics?

The setup of the Kratky method is one of the simplest out there in the world of hydroponic systems. You just need a growing container, some net cups, nutrients, growing media, and the lid to prevent the nutrients from evaporating.

THE KRATKY METHOD: A PASSIVE HYDROPONIC WAY TO GROW PLANTS

If you want to try to get a bit of hydroponic growing happening but don't know where to start, then the Kratky method is for you. It's the sort of passive hydroponics that are an excellent starting point for beginners. It's also an easy, "set and forget" technique that veterans can use to squeeze a bit more out of every forgotten corner. It's the easiest of all the Deep Water Culture techniques, hands down. All you need is a bucket with a hole in the lid, a sunny spot and bit of patience.

Best Plants that Grow Well In Kratky Hydroponics

Lettuce

Lettuce is a perfect starter crop for those new to hydroponic gardening. It was after all one of the crops used to develop this low-maintenance technique. I've seen great little units build in re-used coffee containers or the like. Compact varieties are ideal to put in a small container and allow you to get the most from your growing space.

Basil

There's no such thing as too much basil. You can grow kratky basil in a rig made from as little as Mason jar on a kitchen counter. I've even struck root off store bough basil bunches to get started. They're unbelievably vigorous plants and delicious too.

Cucumber

If you've got a lot more room to play with cucumber is a great choice. They want larger containers and space to spread. Those glorious vines will also need a trellis or other support. But once they're off and running they'll continue to provide delicious crisp fruit with no need for extra fertilizer along the way.

Cabbage

Like lettuce cabbages thrive under the Kratky method of hydroponic cultivation. They're good candidates for sequential plantings a few weeks apart, and growing indoors is a great way to keep them pest free too.

Peppers

I generally don't recommend you use the Kratky method to grow heavy feeders like tomatoes and peppers. It's just too easy to under-nourish during the critical flowering phase if you've locked their water and nutrient solution inside a big box. But I make exception for peppers. If you're gunning for truly fiery, fruity peppers you can control inputs best if you grow the plants with the Kratky method.

Keeping each set of roots in its own closed environment means you can supply the right amount of nutrients to please each plant without neglecting the others.

Benefits of Using the Kratky System

Flexible

The uses for this sort of passive system is only limited by your imagination. Just about any closed container can hold plant food. Small rigs, large ones, single crop or salad tables all work off the same principle. It's such an easy way to grow it'll adapt to almost all situations. No matter what you want to grow there's a way to make Kratky work for you.

Cheap

If you're new to hydroponics the cost of startup can be daunting. While I love my Aerogarden not everyone can afford such a sophisticated system. But everyone has a right to fresh food and Kratky hydroponics are easy to set up with very little investment. If you have access to good light, rainwater, an old tub and some plant cuttings you can grow plants with the Kratky method. There's no running costs for pumps and filters.

Once you've added a nutrient solution you're essentially done. About the only real investment an electrical conductivity meter and they are increasingly affordable online.

Environmentally Friendly

Kratky is a supremely environmentally friendly type of hydroponic system. Recycled containers hold hydroponic nutrient solutions just as well as purpose made. Baskets and substrate like clay pellets can be reused time and time again. I've even heard of people cutting slits in Dixie cups for baskets too! It's thrifty and puts trash to good use. The environmental benefits don't end there.

Because the water solution is sealed it limits evaporation and saves a lot of water from waste.

You only need to water once all season. Even drip irrigation systems will go through more than that. Lastly if you're lucky enough to have a well lit spot you don't have to power anything at all. Even here in the Great White North I can cut my energy input down to a high efficiency LED grow light.

How To Set Up A Kratky Hydroponic System

You will need:

- ✓ Plastic container or tub with lid.
- ✓ Mesh basket
- ✓ Growing medium
- ✓ Nutrient solution
- ✓ Water
- ✓ Seedling or rooted cutting
- ✓ EC/pH meter (optional)

Step One

- ✓ Start by preparing your medium. If you've opted to use clay pellets, soak in clean water overnight. Rinse coir to clear any extra salts.
- ✓ While your medium is soaking prepare your container. Opaque containers are best as they prevent algae in the roots. Wash and rinse thoroughly and allow to dry.
- ✓ Cut a hole in your lid. It must be cut to fit your basket so that it sits firmly but allows it to hang comfortably below.

Step Two

- ✓ Once your medium is ready to go, mix up your solution.
- ✓ For beginners, a commercial nutrient solution blends designed for leafy greens is good. Always mix the nutrients according to instructions. Tap water is generally fine but

if you're concerned distilled water is okay too.

✓ Just be sure to follow the instructions. The specific amount of water listed on the label should give you a good pH and the right nutrient concentration.

✓ If you want to use a more general purpose liquid fertilizer check the pH and electrical conductivity before you add plants. An electric EC and pH meter won't be hard to find online and they'll help you keep a close eye on any future hydro experiments too.

✓ Once the solution is prepared fill the container leaving the depth of the basket clear at the top, and pop the lid in place.

Step Three

✓ Plant your seedling in the moist medium. Ensure the roots are well distributed inside.

Step Four

✓ Place your basket in the lid so the bottom is just touching the solution. At most it should not be submerged no more than a quarter of an inch.

Step Five

✓ Place your newly built Kratky rig in a well lit area. If you've opted to grow away from natural light position your grow light too.

The Best Growing Medium For The Kratky Method

I love clay pebbles for Kratky rigs. They provide great support to plants and keep them both hydrated and well aerated. Clay pebbles don't rot and drop debris into your tank. Once you harvest your vegetables you can wash and reuse them for the next round too. There's a lot to recommend them! That said clay pebbles can be a bit expensive in some areas. Coco coir or perlite work well too.

Disadvantages of the Kratky Hydroponic Method

Limits to Size

While Kratky is a flexible method, you do have a hard upper limit for size. It really isn't practical to try and manage huge tubs of water. My back is sore just thinking about it. Not to mention the hazards of having that kind of weight on structures like decks or balconies. Ebb and flow or drip irrigation is better for truly expansive systems.

Limits To Time Frame

Kratky is best for shorter lifespan crops that are harvested at the end of the growing season. Long-lived types of plants will drop the water level in the reservoir down to nothing over the course of their lives. Crops like hydroponic blueberries are going to run out of water or nutrients long before they're ready to harvest.

Root Problems

A closed dark tub filled with motionless water and nutrients is a paradise to root diseases like Pythium and Phytopthora . While there's no greater risk of disease in simple hydroponic rigs like these it does make it far harder to spot and treat root problems.

Can I Top Up My Kratky Nutrient Solution?

It's perfectly fine to refill your reservoir if your plant empties it before the growing season is done. Warm weather makes for thirsty plants that substantially drop the water level in the tank. You may also have just misjudged how much you needed or wound up with a real grower of a plant stripping the nutrient level. If you do refill you need to be aware of the oxygen needs of the root system.

You can't just fill the reservoir to the top as you did at the start. Aim to cover about half of the total root mass. This will keep the nutrient level just right while providing roots the air they need to thrive. You also need to really check the EC and PH. High temperatures can also cause your solution to become too concentrated. It pays to test before you close that lid again.

Is Kratky Similar To Deep Water Culture (DWC)?

Kratky is indeed a Deep Water Culture hydroponic method. Generally when folks talk about Deep Water Culture they mean more complex builds with filtration and aeration systems. These are 'active' hydroponic systems. Kratky setups are a passive hydroponic system. Also called non-circulating hydroponic systems, they don't require pumps, filters or air stones.

The simple system exploits the way plants exhale water taken from the roots into the air. As the water level drops it provides oxygen to the root zone that only increases as the entire plant gets larger.

Hydroponics: How To Grow Food with a Kratky Jar

What is a Kratky jar?

Kratky jarThe Kratky method of hydroponics was discovered by Bernard Kratky, Emeritus Horticulturalist at the University of Hawaii. It's a passive method, requiring no pumps, fans, or anything fancy. Kratky jars can be made from just about anything, from a standard Mason jar to an old plastic creamer bottle. Some Kratky systems are very large and fancy, utilizing large totes or tanks.

The only limit is your imagination and what's in your possession. This method is ideal for apartment & condo dwellers since it requires so little space or equipment. It's also very adaptable and can be used to grow anything from greens & herbs to tomatoes, peppers, squashes, and cucumbers. (It's not well suited to root crops, however, since the vegetables will tend to break the reservoir.)

The basic setup is very simple

The little plant is suspended in a net pot containing some kind of structural component, such as rock wool, coco coir, or peat moss. The reservoir is filled with nutrient-containing water, and there should be an air space in the jar. Most plants don't like wet feet, and they need oxygen just as much as we do. The plant roots will grow down into the solution as they feed, making the air space larger as the nutrient solution is used up.

What do you need to set up a Kratky jar?

The reservoir can be just about anything, as noted above. The size of the reservoir will be a factor in what exactly can be grown in your Kratky jar. If you're using a Mason jar or creamer bottle, you'll want to grow smaller things like greens, herbs, and micro-tomatoes. If you're using a large tote with holes cut into the top, you can grow full-size tomatoes, taro, cucumbers, eggplants, and even strawberries.

I'm growing micro-tomatoes in mine. I'll likely expand as I learn more and become more comfortable with the method. Also, note that covering the jar, so light doesn't grow algae in it isn't a bad idea if you're using a clear glass reservoir. Net pots come in many sizes, and which size you'll need depends on the size of your reservoir. Wide mouth Mason jars will require a 3" pot.

I made my first Kratky jar in a 1/2 gallon Ball jar using a 4" pot, cut down to fit and held in place by the jar ring. I was determined to use only what I had on hand and buy nothing, so I had to adapt a bit. Whatever works, right? The net pot is necessary so the roots can grow freely into the solution. A standard plant pot won't work for this purpose.

Grow media is very easy to acquire, or you can make your own. As noted above, rock wool and coco coir are the most common media but far from the only choices. Rock wool can be expensive but can be reused, ditto coco coir. The media holds the plant upright. It gives no nutrients and serves no other purpose, so in theory, just about anything will do as long as it's not toxic to the system.

Perlite or packing peanuts are even workable as long as they can be kept in the pot. Mesh or even pantyhose can hold the media as long as the roots can grow through it. Similar parameters apply to using kitchen sponges, though please note you don't want the sponges with soap or other chemicals for this use.

As long as they're not too heavy for the plant roots to grow through, it's an option. I chose long-fiber sphagnum moss since it's what I had on hand and stuffed it into my net pot, tight but not too tight.

What kind of nutrient solution do you need?

Many standard hydroponics mixes contain NPK plus calcium, magnesium, and iron. Remember, however, that plants require ten essential nutrients, not six. While plants can be grown using the standard mix, they'll grow better if a few more of the essentials are present, such as boron, manganese, copper, and zinc.

There are a number of excellent commercial mixes, such as Masterblend International, or you can very easily make your own using compost from your own pile in the form of compost tea. Simply add a shovel full or two to a five-gallon bucket of water, let it sit for three days, strain out the sediment, and use. Suspend the plant in the reservoir such that the roots touch the nutrient solution.

This is a very important point! The nutrients won't do the plant any good if the roots aren't absorbing nutrients, right?

Another component is lighting.

Windows are fine as long as the light is strong enough. Grow lights are a great option, and combining the two is perfectly acceptable. I placed my Kratky jar by an East-facing window beneath a single T5 grow light, and my micro tomato seems to be quite happy there. LCD panels are certainly an option as well. Note that this is the only part of the Kratky system that requires power.

Other than this, Kratky is a completely passive system. A pH meter is totally optional but a nice thing to have, nonetheless. Most vegetable plants prefer a pH in the 6.5-6.8 range, and some plants, such as strawberries and blueberries, prefer an environment even more acidic. If you have a pH meter handy, you can better help to ensure that you are giving your little plants the optimum environment for maximum growth.

So that's all there is to it!

All you need is a reservoir, a net pot, nutrients, and good lighting. There are no fans or pumps to worry about, so the power going out isn't as deadly to this system as it is to others. And that's not the only benefit of passive hydroponics! For those with very short growing seasons, such as myself, this system can be used to provide fresh greens and other goodies through the winter, when those things are outrageously expensive to buy.

Smaller reservoirs can turn unproductive tabletops into food-producing areas, and I believe that any item I can grow is one less thing I need to buy at the grocery store! Hydroponics can add a layer to your food production system, and Kratky jars are the easiest way to get your feet wet if you've never worked with this particular method. A single jar can expand into totes worth of food, produced right in your own space.

This method is suitable for apartments and condos, where space is at a premium and yard gardening may not be an option. Keep the weight of a water-filled tote in mind before you put it on your lanai, however! Most lanai aren't built to take a lot of weight. But within parameters, it's very easy, so why not give it a try? You may be pleasantly surprised at what you can grow!

And while you're at it, make a plan to use or preserve all of that fresh produce. The Seasonal Kitchen Companion contains not only fun trivia but the basics of canning, freezing, and dehydrating anything you can't eat right away. Since city dwellers such as myself also buy from the farmer's market and my CSA, preserving what I have for winter eating is a must!

HOW TO GROW CANNABIS USING

THE KRATKY METHOD OF

HYDROPONICS

Growing hydroponic cannabis isn't rocket science. With a bit of patience and understanding, you can grow dank buds like some of the most experienced growers out there. Whether you want to switch to hydroponics or are just starting, you can grow amazing plants, provided you understand the science behind it all.

Rather than aping others, it's best to understand the plant and master the technique required to give you the best results. Hydroponics has several variants, and each one of them differs from one another. While you can grow cannabis with any variant, starting with the easiest one at first makes sense. In this guide book, we will explore one of the simplest hydroponics methods, called the Kratky method.

Other techniques require energy, lots of space, pumps, and tubes to grow plants, but the Kratky method is a hands-off way of growing cannabis — a set-it-and-forget-it system. Sounds interesting, right? So, let's get started — here's a guide on growing cannabis using the Kratky method.

The Kratky Method

The Kratky method was introduced by BA Kratky, who was a student at the University of Huawei at the time. This method is very similar to DWC or Deep Water Culture — another hydroponic technique to grow plants; however, the Kratky process doesn't require a pump to function. In addition, you don't even have to make any changes to the reservoir's nutrients! And, as if that's not enough, it's one of the cheapest systems because it doesn't require special equipment.

Here's a simple diary displaying the Kratky method from start to finish This low-maintenance hydroponic method to grow cannabis can set you free from the hustle of growing cannabis. All you have to do is:

- ✓ Place a plant in a net pot
- ✓ Fill the tank with nutrient solution
- ✓ Place the net pot at the top of the reservoir
- ✓ Harvest the buds when it's all done!

I can almost hear you wondering whether this is too good to be true. Most beginners and even some experienced growers shy away from hydroponics because it all sounds so complicated. Soil is a little more forgiving where you get a chance to help your plants in distress, but hydroponics can be brutal at times. A small mistake in the pH can ruin things. Remember, you will need to maintain pH and other essential things even with Kratky, but it won't be as complex as other methods.

Not to mention that you won't be spending as much money as well. To put it simply, this method works amazingly well if you're planning to grow just a few plants. The system can survive on its own for a few weeks, but you may have to interfere at times to check the water levels and pH readings.

How does the Kratky method work?

As mentioned already, it's very similar to DWC, except that it doesn't need other electronic devices or wicks and pumps. No matter what method you use, plants require water, oxygen, light, and nutrients to grow. While the system takes care of oxygen, you will have to supply both macro and micronutrients and light for the plants to grow to their maximum potential. The Kratky technique supplies all these essential ingredients easily with a little help from you:

✓ Nutrients – Just like other hydroponic systems, you will need to add the nutrients to the reservoir containing water.

- ✓ Fill the net pot with the chosen growing media such as rockwool or clay pebbles, and insert the plant into the net pot.
- ✓ Hang the net pot supported by a lid at the top of the container.
- ✓ Do not submerge the roots entirely in water. There must be an air gap between the roots and the water, so the plant gets adequate oxygen.

Over time, as the plants continue to grow, the reservoir's water level decreases as the plants absorb it all, and you may have to intervene if the plants aren't ready to be harvested yet. The Kratky method is so simple yet efficient because it provides water and oxygen effortlessly. As the cultivator, your job is to provide the lighting and the nutrients. Compared to other hydroponic techniques, this is the easiest and most efficient method with minimal interference.

In a nutshell, the plant roots absorb the water and pass the nutrients to the plant. Water depletion then creates air or oxygen for the plant to breathe in. And since cannabis is a fast-growing plant, they grow best in the Kratky hydroponic system — by the time the water gets absorbed, the plant is ready to harvest!

What do you need for the Kratky method?

The Kratky method requires some basic tools such as:

Reservoir or container: The reservoir size depends on the size of the plant. Start with compact plants that are easy to maintain instead of jumping to growing monstrous plants on the first try. If you plan to grow a small plant, even a milk jar will work, but you will need bigger containers if you grow strains that tend to grow very big. In addition, your first project will give you an idea of the size for the next try.

Lid: A plastic or styrofoam lid protects your plant from diseases, pests, and water from evaporating. Ensure you keep the lid closed at all times since it protects the plant from diseases and pests and prevents water evaporation. If you purchase a ready-made setup, you can buy the lid; however, if you're setting up a DIY system (we will get to that later), a plastic or styrofoam lid will work just fine. The lid will also support the plant from collapsing as you hang it at the top. Net pots anchor the plant and are usually made from plastic mesh to promote drainage and circulate air.

Grow medium: Grow medium is placed within the net pots. You can use perlite, but I recommend hydroton or clay pebbles since perlite tends to seep through the net pots, making it very messy. Also, make sure you purchase pH-neutral grow media.

Nutrient solution: A regular hydroponic nutrient solution mixed with water works best for the

Kratky method to grow cannabis. Pro tip – If liquid nutrients seem too expensive, you can purchase nutrient kits containing both macro and micronutrients and mix them according to the instructions on the label, making it a lot cheaper for you.

pH control kit: The kit would contain the pH meter and other tools that help you identify and rectify the culture's pH balance. In other words, you will need a solution that increases the pH (pH UP) and another solution that reduces the pH (pH DOWN) along with a pH meter.

Steps to follow

The Kratky method to grow cannabis is relatively easy, and you only need to follow five steps. You can go for a ready-made setup or set one up yourself.

Step 1: Prepare the lid

First, you need to fix the lid on your reservoir. For this, cut the top with a drilling machine or any other tool to create a hole large enough for a net pot to get through.

Step 2: Fill the reservoir with water

Next, fill the reservoir with water. You can use both tap or distilled water, but avoid using dirty or contaminated water at all costs — the water will be stagnant throughout the process, and you don't want it to turn into a pest haven!

Step 3: Prepare the nutrient solution

Add the nutrients one by one to the reservoir and mix the water thoroughly. Or, you can mix the nutrients in another container separately and add it all at once to the reservoir.

Step 4: Check the pH levels

Your Kratky culture is almost ready! Now, it's time to check the pH balance using a pH pen or meter. The reservoir's pH balance should be between 5.8 and 6.2, an ideal range for the cannabis plant.

Adjust pH

If it's not in the suitable range, increase or decrease the pH before proceeding.

Step 5: Plant cannabis

Fill the net pot with growing media and insert your seedling into the pot. Next, place the net pot in the drilled lid of the reservoir. While doing so, ensure some of the roots are exposed to air while its lower parts are in the nutrient solution.

How does the Kratky method work to grow cannabis?

As mentioned already, the Kratky method works on a few basic principles of effortlessly supplying water and oxygen to the plants. This simplistic method allows you to continue your business rather than worrying about the plants. As long as you monitor the pH levels and check the plants for pests, deficiencies, and diseases frequently, you can grow some stunning plants with this method.

Drawbacks

Everything has drawbacks, and the Kratky method is no different. You may encounter some disadvantages, including:

- ✓ The Kratky hydroponic system has many variables, like pH levels and temperatures, affecting the plant's growth.
- ✓ The Kratky method is only suitable for small cannabis cultures. A big culture would require a lot of manual labor in cleaning and preparing the systems, which is not worth it.
- ✓ The method is also prone to pests because of the lack of air stones and stagnant

nutrient solutions, attracting pests like gnats and mosquitoes. So be prepared to deal with pests beforehand.

Summary

The Kratky method to grow cannabis is the perfect way for beginners to get started with growing cannabis. So, if you do things right — use the right kind of tools, water, medium, and nutrients while maintaining stable temperatures and pH, you will grow a healthy cannabis plant right at home. Compared to other methods, the Kratky is by far the easiest. And, even if you take a DIY approach, it shouldn't cost you more than $30-$40 to gather a container, lid, and some water.

THE BEGINNERS GUIDE TO THE

KRATKY METHOD OF HYDROPONICS

Growing vegetables, whether for yourself or a business, can be quite the endeavor. Hydroponics, or the growing of plants without soil, is becoming increasingly popular in our modern world. The Kratky Method is one of the simplest ways of doing this. Here is our step-by-step beginner's guide to the Kratky method of hydroponics:

- ✓ Building Your Reservoir
- ✓ Adding Water and Nutrients
- ✓ Checking the pH
- ✓ Planting & Inserting the Plant
- ✓ Waiting as Your Plant Grows
- ✓ Harvesting Your Plants
- ✓ Rinse & Repeat

Gardeners love the Kratky method of hydroponics because it involves no electricity or attention as the plant grows. Read on to learn how to set your plant up and let them grow, and in a few short weeks, you can have luscious plants ready to eat.

Step by Step Guide to the Kratky Method of Hydroponics

By following these guidelines carefully, anyone can have a garden growing in just a short time with the Kratky method. Before beginning, collect the following supplies:

- ✓ Five-gallon bucket
- ✓ Net pots
- ✓ Uncontaminated water
- ✓ pH test and control kit
- ✓ Hydroponic nutrients
- ✓ Growing medium

Using these materials, you can have a DIY hydroponic setup in just a few hours.

1. Building Your Reservoir

While there are many different ways to make a suitable container for the Kratky method, using a five-gallon bucket is a great place to start. Each five-gallon bucket can hold a plant as it grows to maturity. But, you will need an additional bucket for each plant you want to grow. After procuring your bucket, cut a hole in the center of the lid to the size of your net pots.

Most people choose a 3" pot and, therefore, cut a 3" hole. You can make the hole with a large drill bit or with a small drill bit and saw.

2. Adding Water and Nutrients

Now that the bucket is ready, you need to add the water and nutrients, so the plant has something to drink from. The plants will need good, uncontaminated water. Often, town and city water has a high concentration of particulates that can have a detrimental effect. So, opt for filtered water or buy inexpensive distilled water from your local grocery store.

Next, fill the bucket up with your clean water until it is three inches from the top. Follow the instructions on your hydroponic nutrients bottle to nourish the water. Make sure to stir each nutrient in well.

3. Checking the pH

The pH tells us how acidic or basic a substance is. On a scale from 0 to 14, 7 is considered neutral. For growing leafy greens, the desired pH is between 5.5 and 6.5. This slightly basic solution produces optimum performance for the root system. To check the pH, you will need a pH test kit. This will allow you to test the pH, but it will also give you precise chemicals to raise or lower the pH as needed.

Most pH tests will be a small strip that you dip into the water. Then, it will change color to blue, green, yellow, or red. By comparing the test strip color to a provided chart, you can determine the pH and adjust accordingly.

4. Planting & Inserting the Plant

The Kratky method is a hands-off method once you get the system going. This means that it is simple, but also is not able to keep up with plants that have high nutrient demands. So, it is best to focus on growing leafy greens, such as lettuce, spinach, or arugula. Start your seed or a small plant in the growing medium in the net pot. One of the best choices of growing medium for hydroponics is clay pebbles.

As a natural and pH-neutral element, it can provide a clean and healthy growing environment for your plant. Once your seed or plant has started growing in the medium, insert the net pot and plant into the lid of the bucket. The nutrient-dense water should cover the bottom third of the net pot. This will allow it to nourish the plant and keep the medium moist while it is still small.

The water level will decrease as the plant grows, but the plant's roots will follow the water at the same rate. This hands-off method keeps air circulating among the roots as the water level drops, and it allows the plant to keep getting water and food as needed.

5. Waiting as Your Plant Grows

Perhaps the most challenging part is waiting for the Kratky method to do its magic. Leave the plant somewhere warm (generally room temperature) with good sunlight, or a grow light. As there is no moving water in this method, it is vital to protect your plant from insects and changing temperatures. The most common pests found sneaking around these pots are mosquitoes, crickets, grasshoppers, and spiders.

To keep these pests minimized, make sure there is no standing water or other damp spots around. This typically isn't an issue indoors but keep an eye out. Also, it is crucial not to let any rain get into the bucket. This could drown the plant's roots or adjust the carefully curated pH levels. If able, put a roof, such as a greenhouse, around your system.

6. Harvesting Your Plants

Harvesting your plants is the exciting part! While you can choose precisely when to harvest, make sure the plant has water at all times. If the water runs out, you can add enough to touch the bottom three to four inches of roots. Most people choose to harvest before the first batch of water is completely gone, though. Smaller greens, like baby spinach and arugula, are very nutrient-dense and tender, too.

7. Rinse & Repeat

There is stagnant water in the Kratky method, so the pots must be sanitized in between growing cycles. If you kept your pots in a greenhouse and there were no signs of pests or bacteria growing, you can do between three to five cycles before having to sanitize. Instead, a good rinse before repeating is all you would need. If, however, you began to suspect any bacteria or had any issues with growth, it is critical to sanitize the bucket before restarting.

To do this, dilute bleach according to the bottle directions and sanitize both the bucket, lid, and net pot. Let them dry completely before beginning again.

Pros and Cons of the Kratky Method

The Kratky method is a simple way to get started growing plants with hydroponics, but every method comes with advantages and disadvantages. Here are some we have found:

Pros

- ✓ Energy-efficient. No electricity is needed to keep water or air moving.
- ✓ Hands-off. Whether you have a heavy work schedule or want to go on vacation, the

plants will continue to grow even if you do not attend to them.

✓ Super simple. The Kratky method is an excellent introduction to hydroponics.

Cons

✓ Attracts pests. The stagnant water is hard to resist for many unwanted critters.

✓ Only useful on a small scale. Once you have too many buckets going, it can be cumbersome to regularly clean and sanitize them from the stagnant water.

✓ Individualized variables to control. Checking and adjusting every single bucket's pH and nutrients can be time-consuming.

Now You Can Grow with the Kratky Method

In a few short hours, you can have a garden growing without any soil or upkeep. This is why the ingenious Kratky method has gained so much momentum over the years. This is an excellent project for someone hoping to supplement their grocery bill or start a CSA.

CONCLUSION

Well, as we reach the end of our journey through explaining the Kratky method of hydroponics, it is quite clear – this is one of the easiest systems for indoor growing. It requires minimum effort, and you can get your favorite leafy greens and veggies ready for your salad or upcoming cooking endeavors quite fast. The Kratky system lets you use simple items like a mason jar to grow plants that are small enough to fit inside.

So, it's the perfect introduction to more complex hydroponic systems, and one of the go-to options for home growers! I love a completely passive system and the Kratky is the easiest to set up and use. It provides everything that my plants will need over their lifespan right at the start. Once they're going I don't need to check much at all and I can leave them alone until they're ready to harvest. It's "set and forget" at its finest.

I've had great success with leafy greens and might just branch out into trickier crops like hydroponic strawberries. Experimenting is half the fun even with the most basic hydroponic techniques. Hopefully, this beginner's guide has given you the boost you need to get started. Feel free to experiment with other containers to maximize your plant and leafy green output!

Printed in Great Britain
by Amazon